# BEAR
# COLORING BOOK

Get FREE printable coloring pages and discounted book prices sent straight to your e-mail inbox every week!

Sign up at:

## www.adultcoloringworld.net

# PREVIEWS:

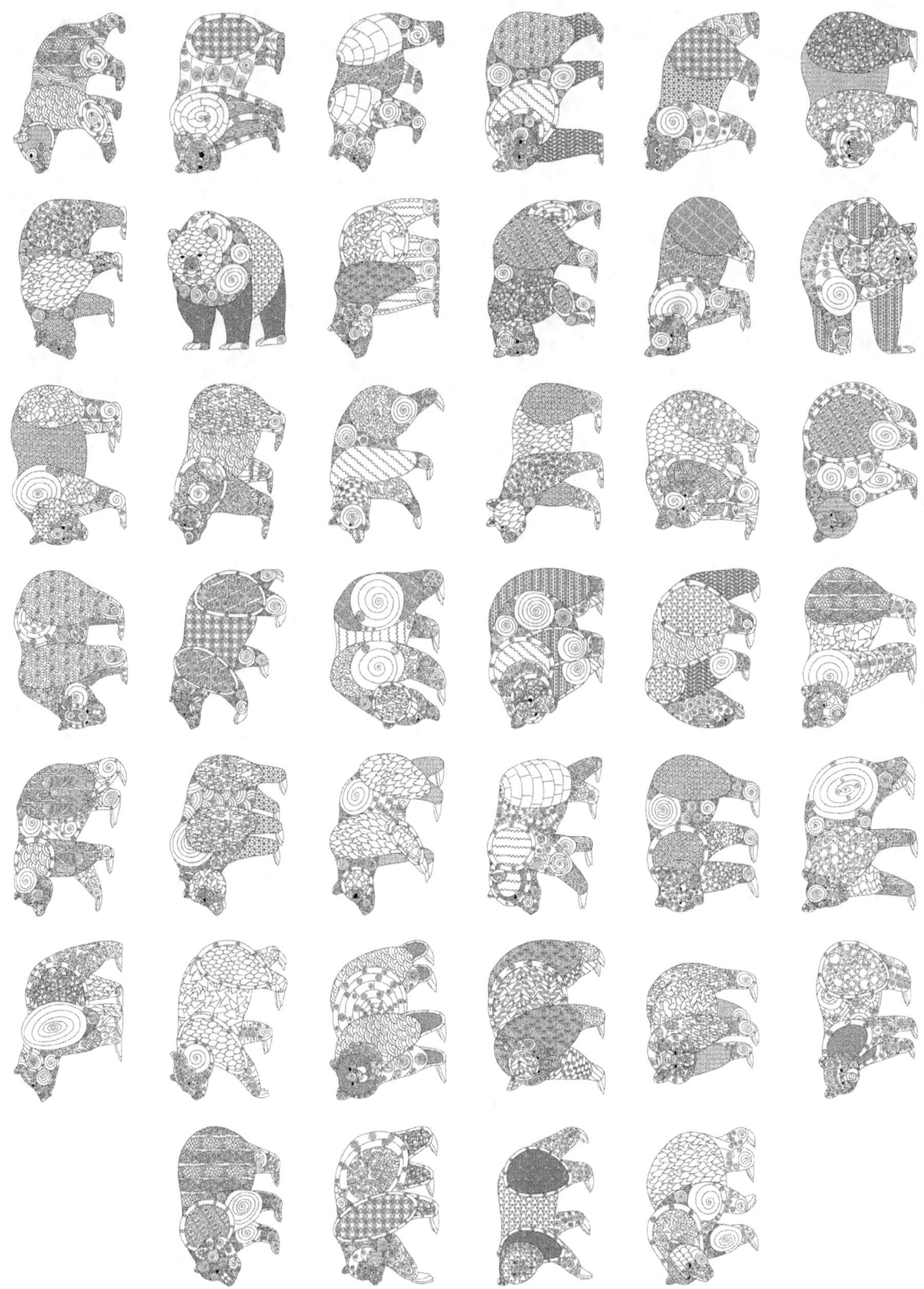

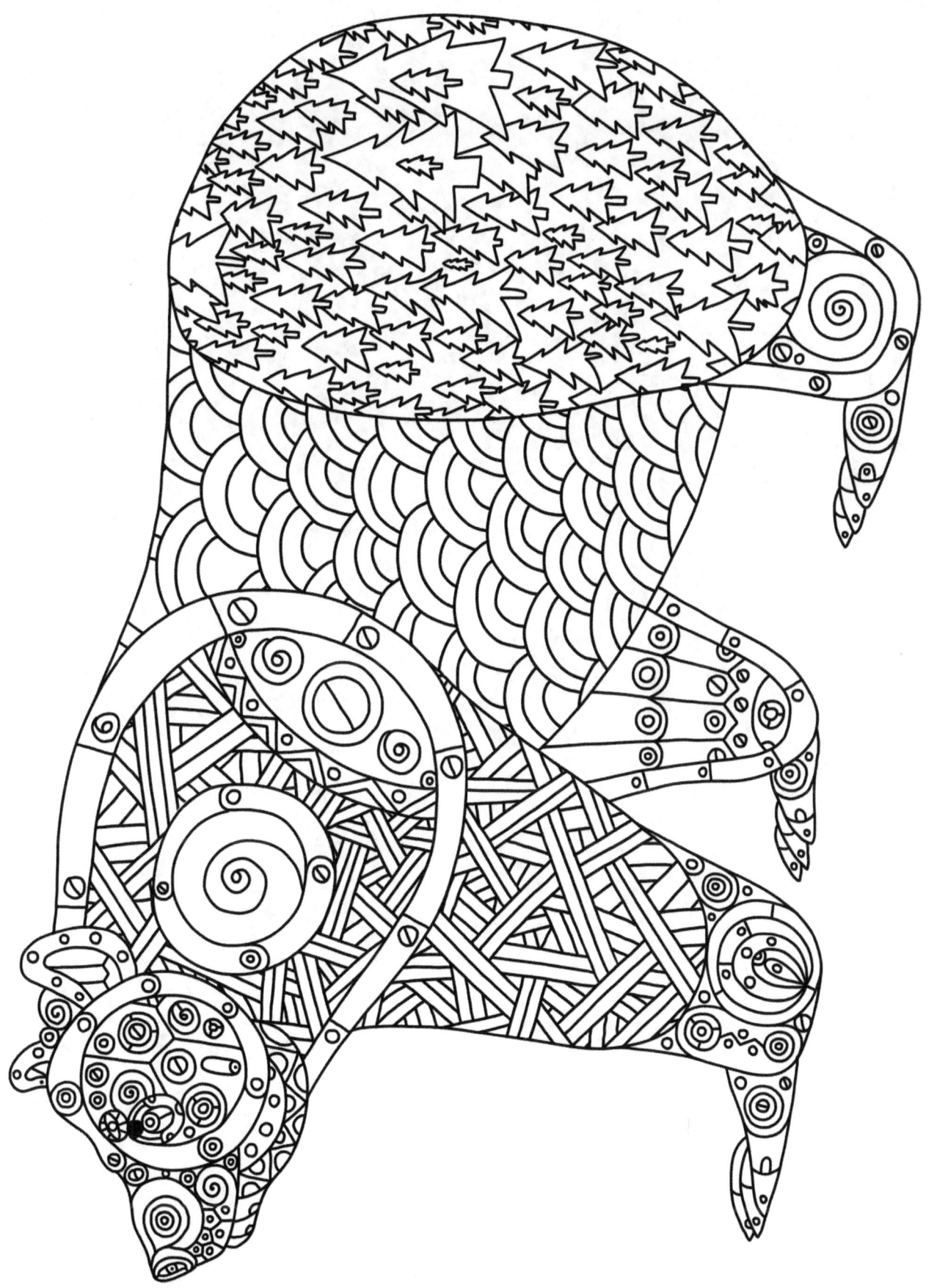

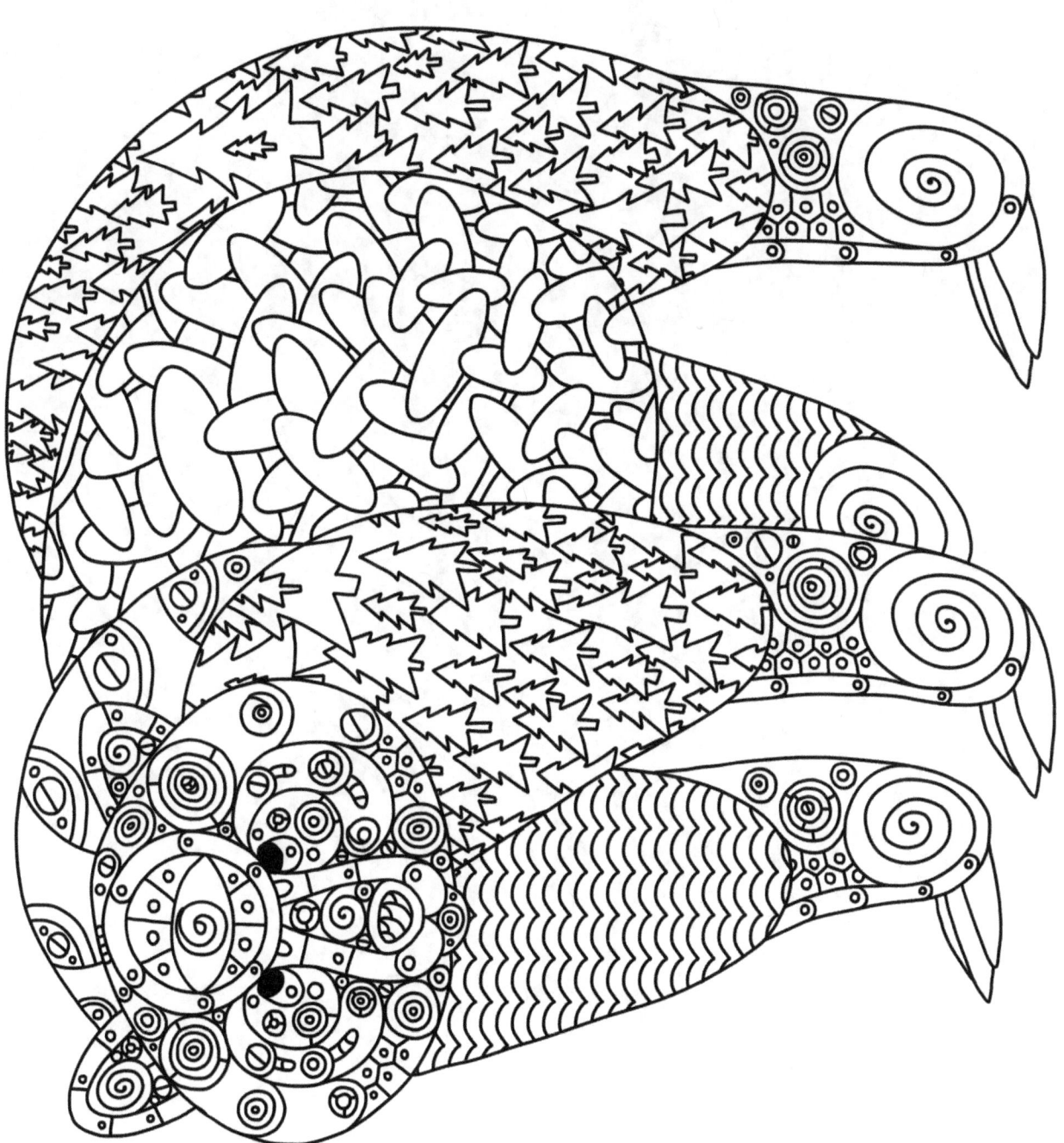

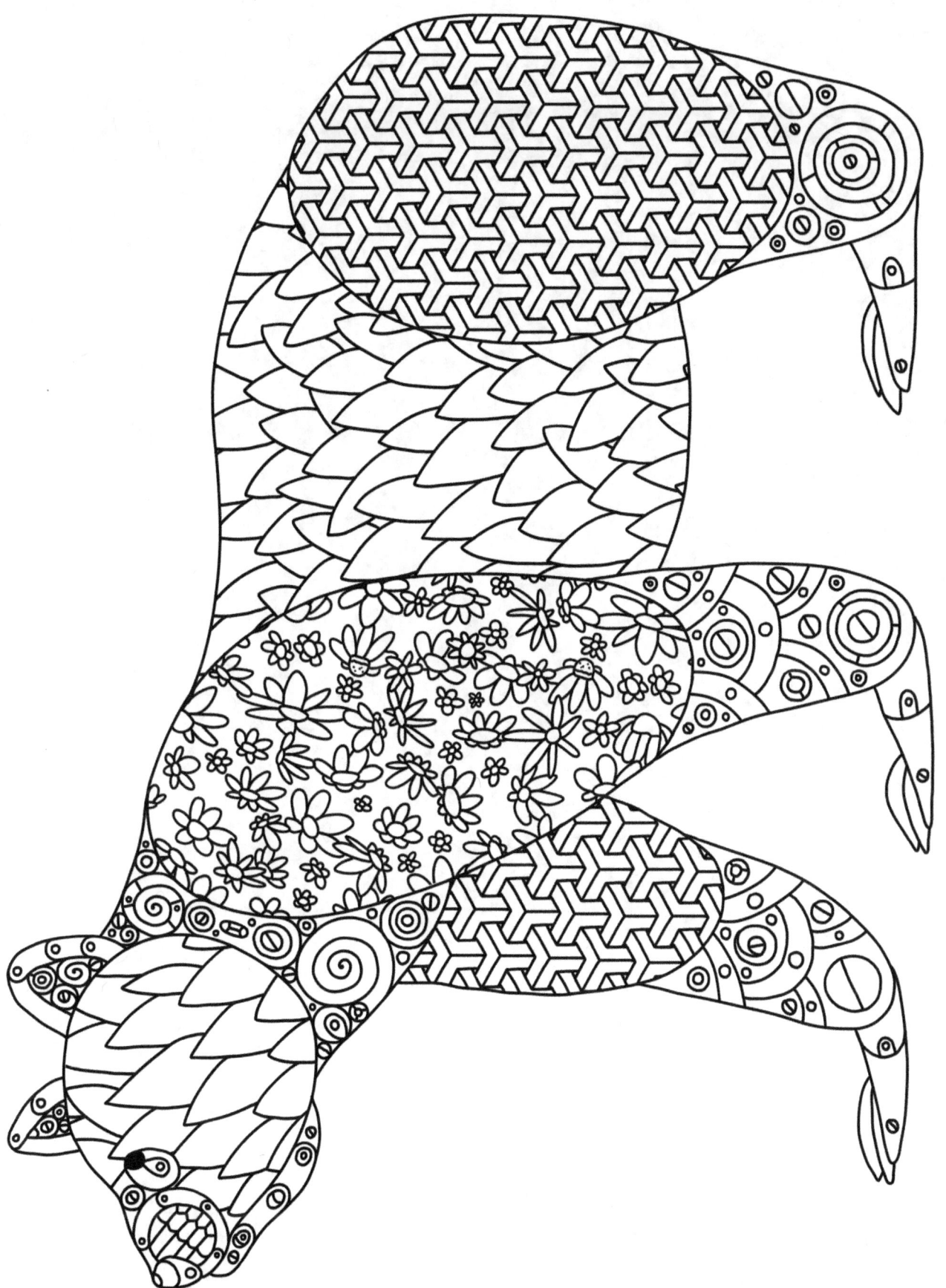

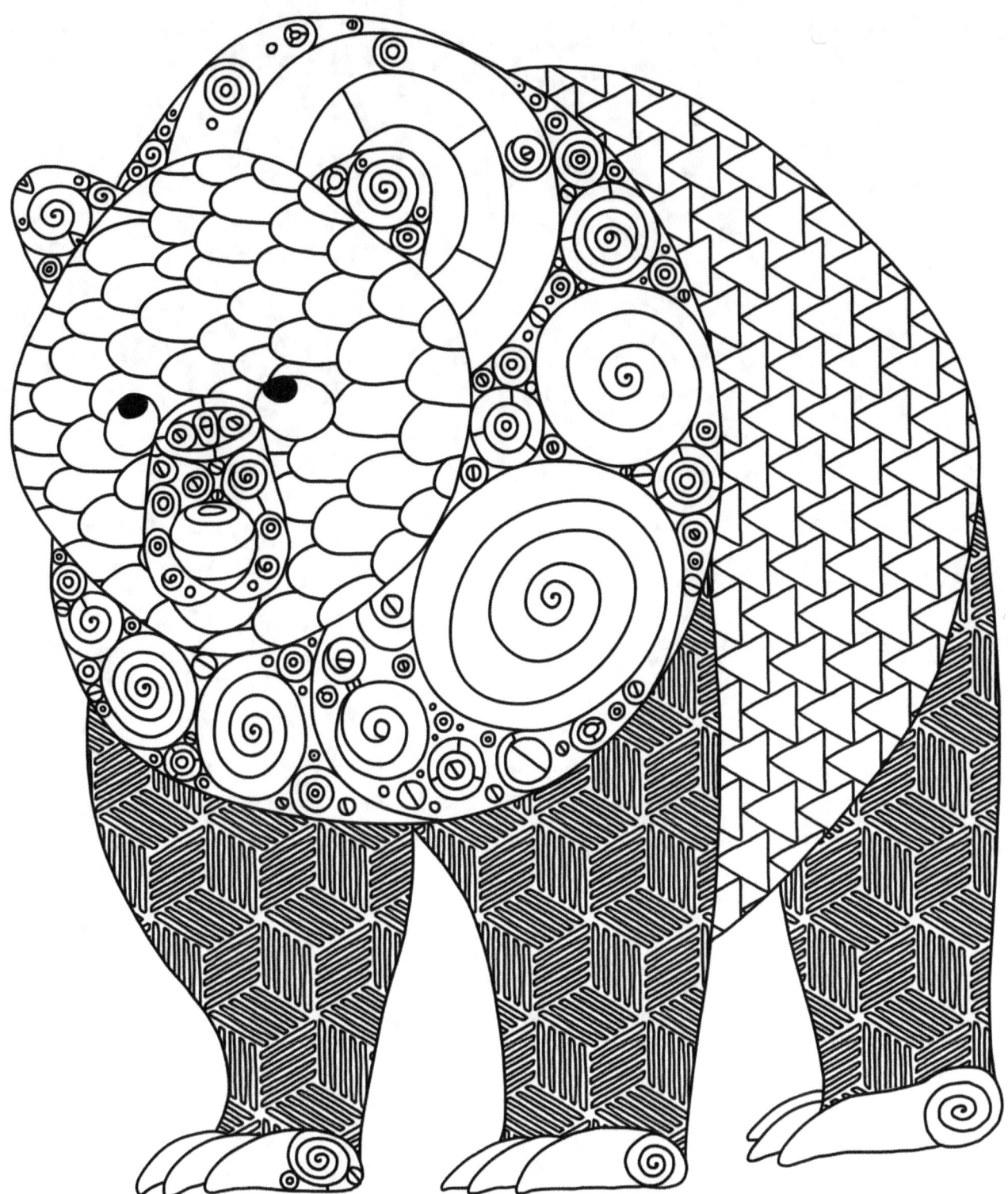

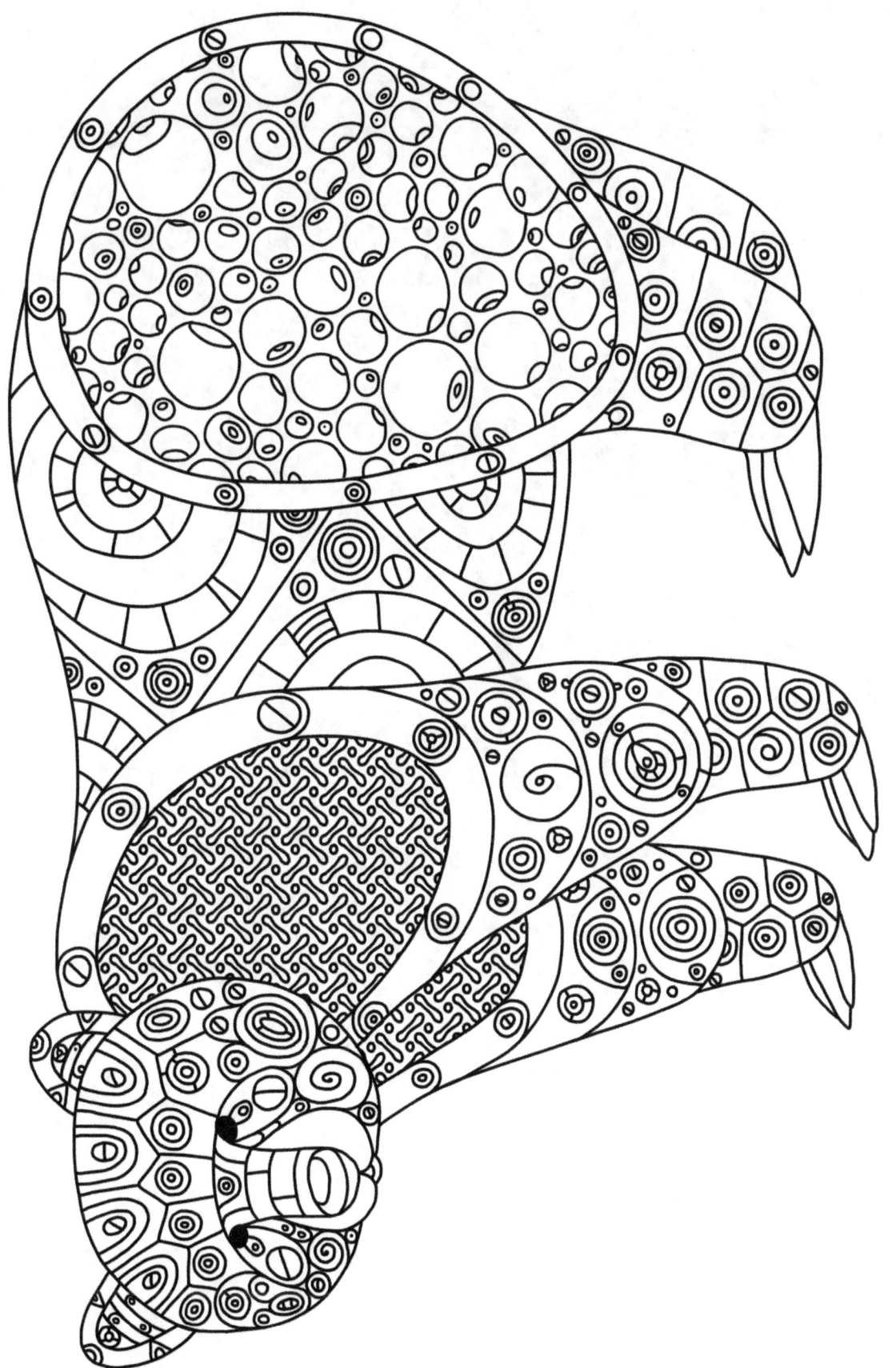

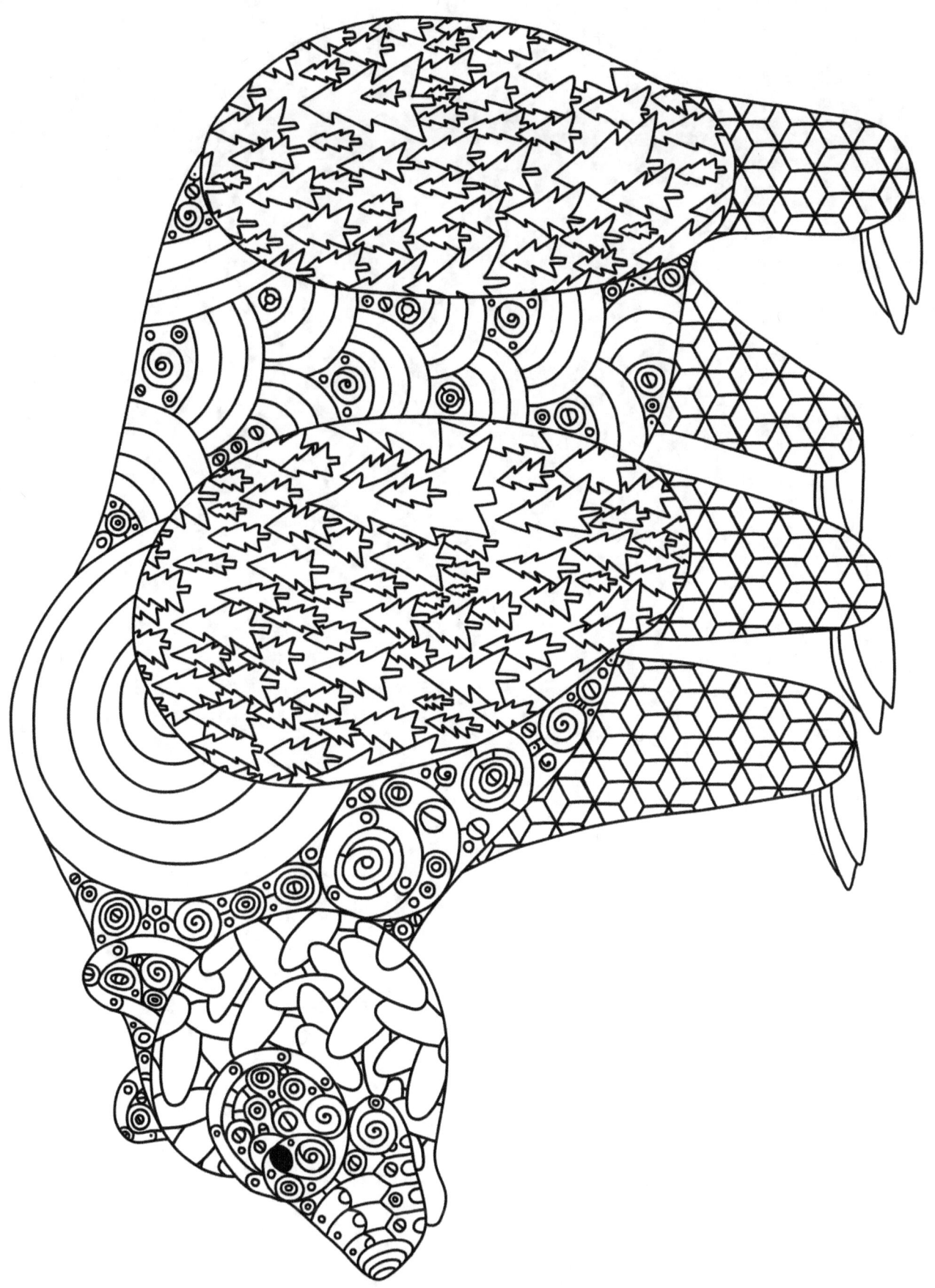

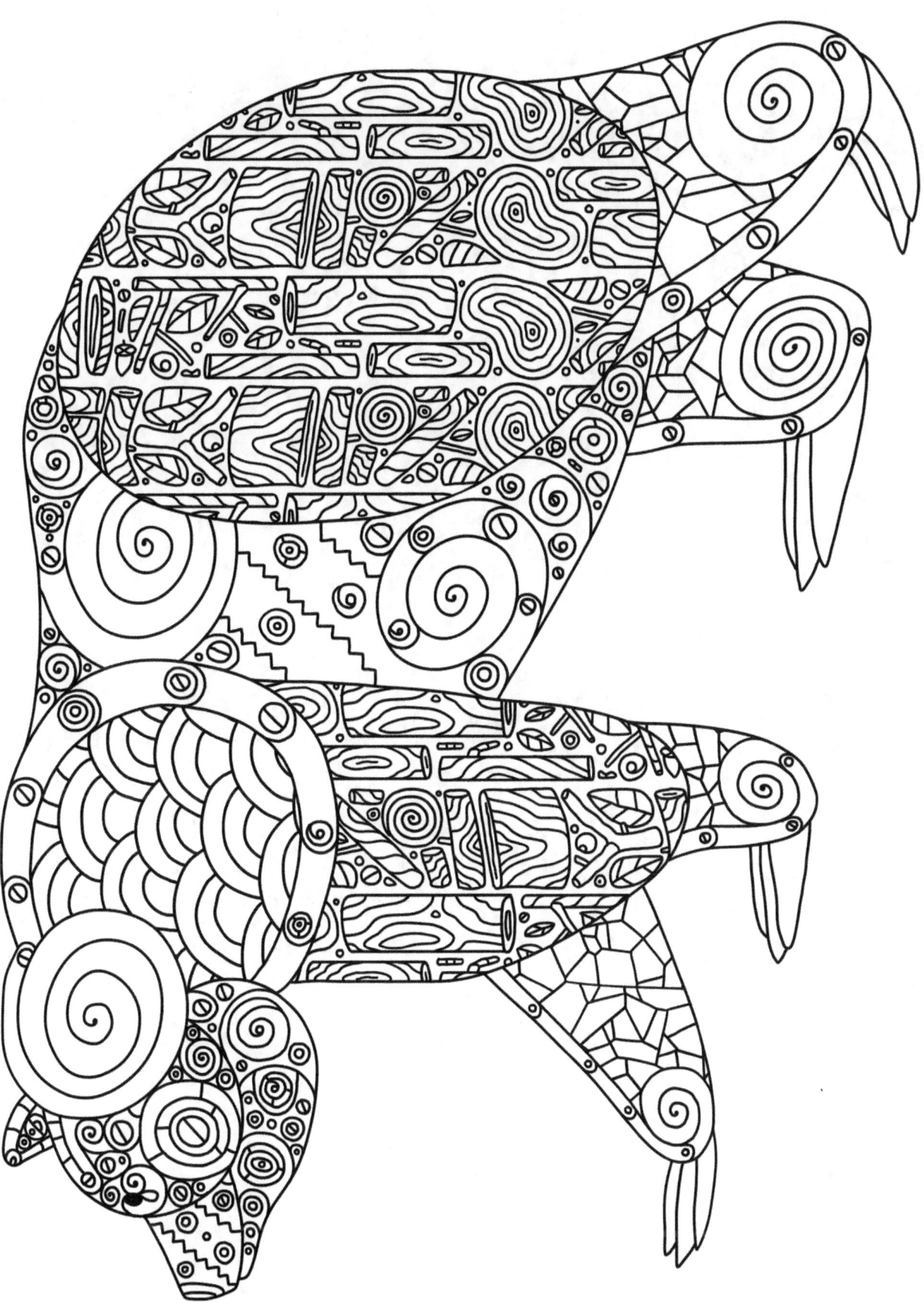

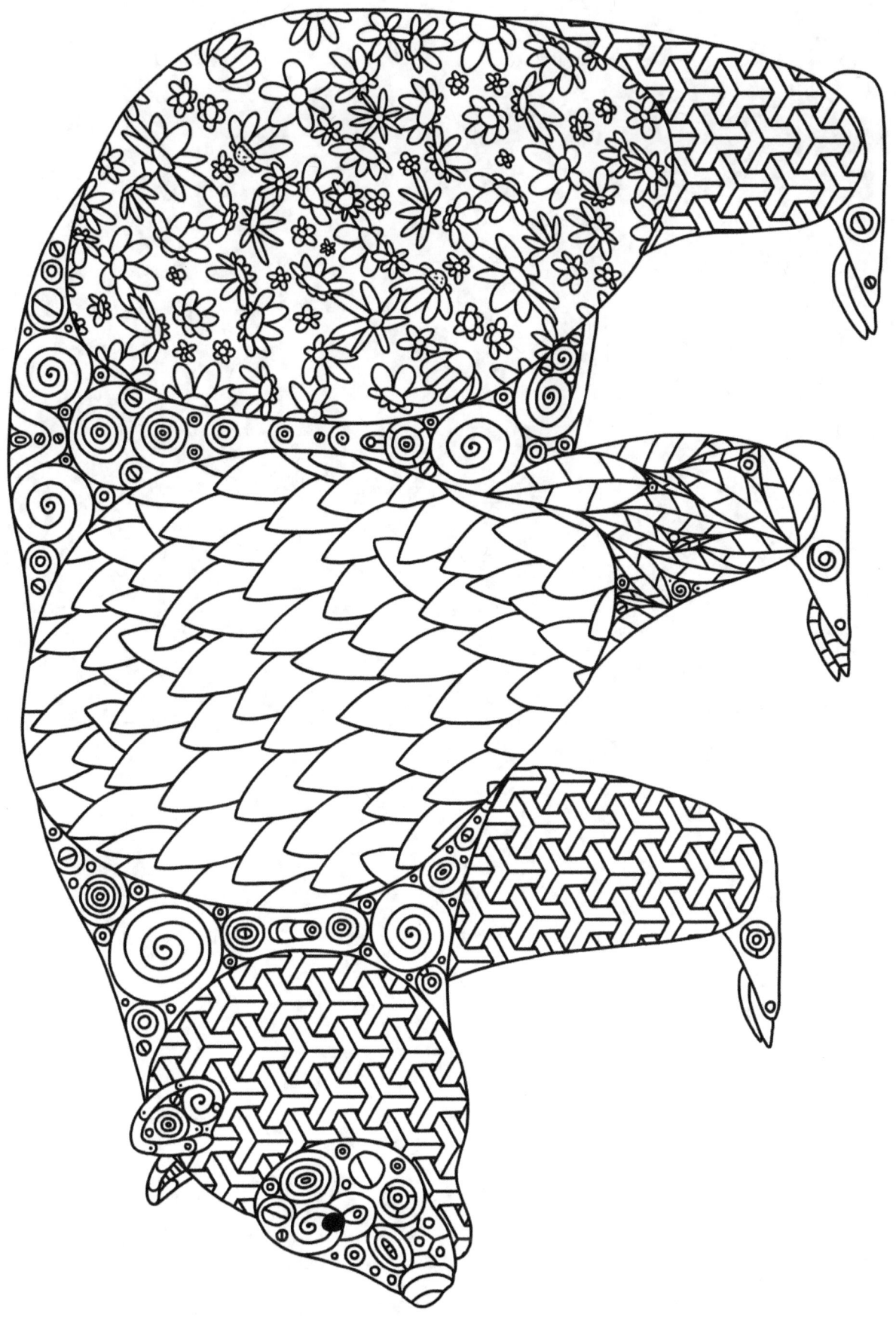

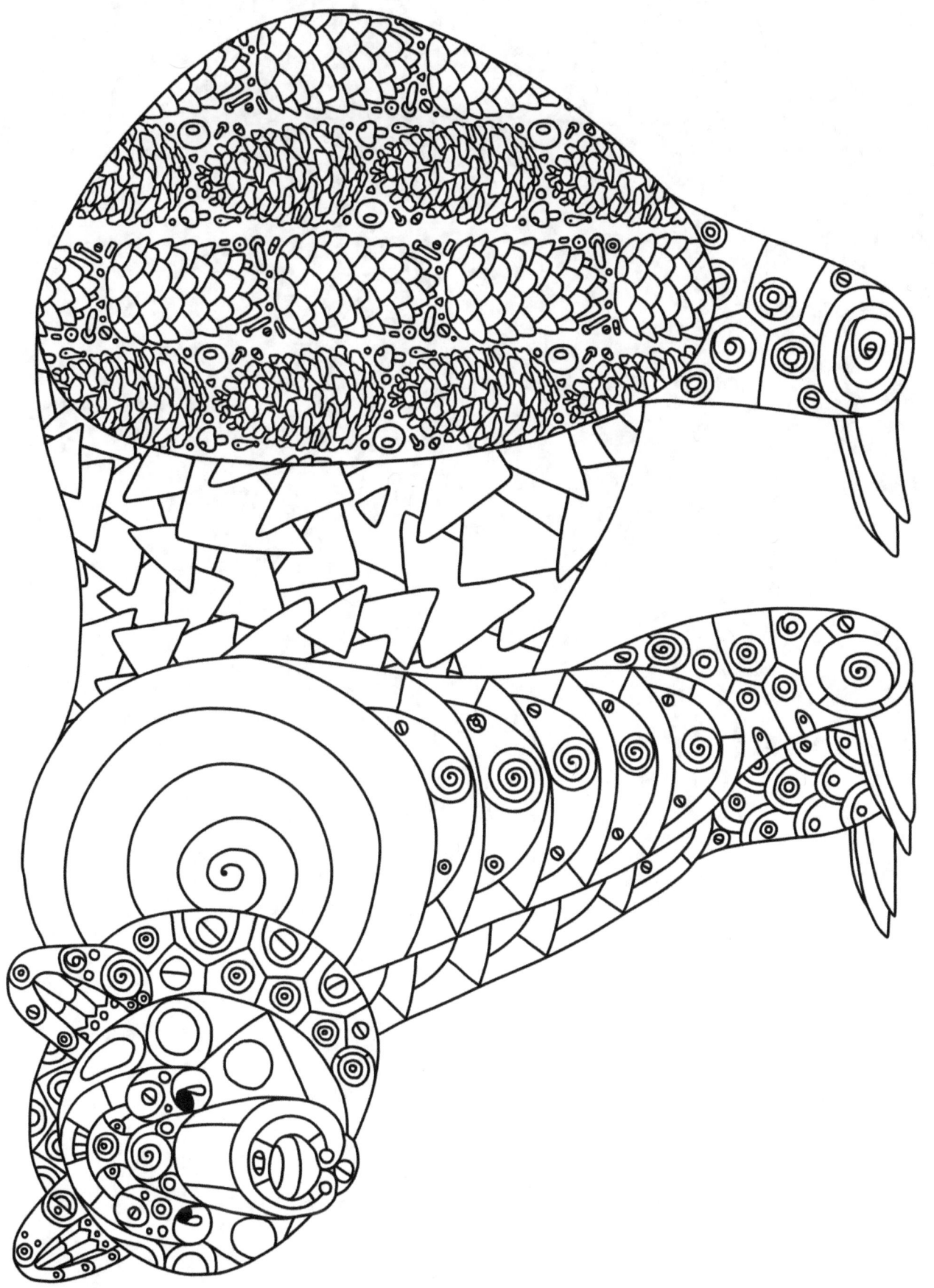

# COLOR TEST PAGE

# COLOR TEST PAGE

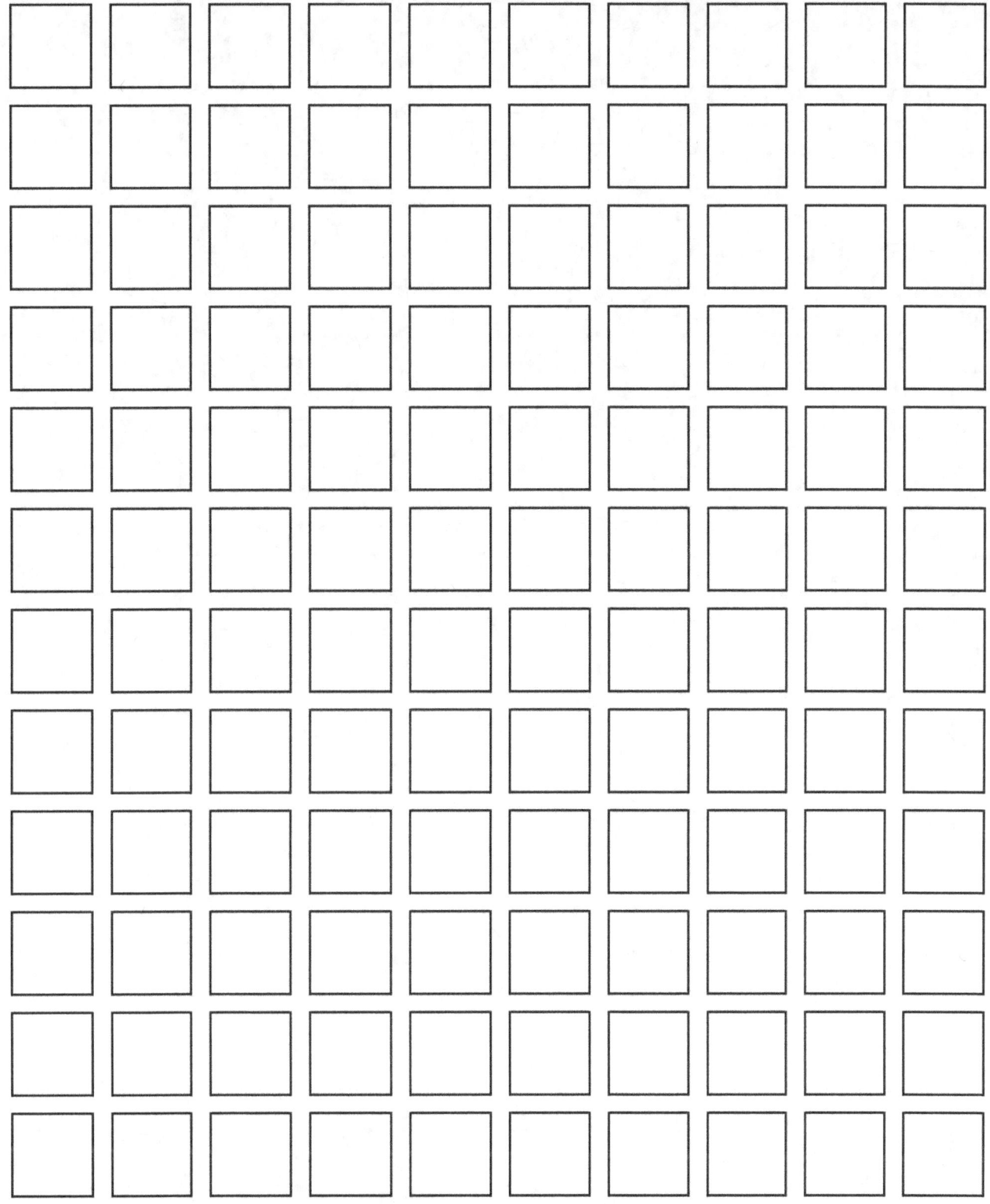

www.ingramcontent.com/pod-product-compliance
Lightning Source LLC
Chambersburg PA
CBHW051947280526
45789CB00009B/3206